MARTIN LUTHER KING, JR.

COLEEN DEGNAN-VENESS

Level 3

Series Editors: Andy Hopkins and Jocelyn Potter

Pearson Education Limited
Edinburgh Gate, Harlow,
Essex CM20 2JE, England
and Associated Companies throughout the world.

ISBN-10: 0-582-77956-1
ISBN-13: 978-0-582-77956-3

First published by Penguin Books 2003

3 5 7 9 10 8 6 4

Text copyright © Coleen Degnan-Veness 2003

The moral rights of the author have been asserted
All rights reserved

Typeset by Pantek Arts Ltd, Maidstone, Kent
Set in 11/15pt Sabon MT
Printed in China
SWTC/03

Published by Pearson Education Limited in association with
Penguin Books Ltd, both companies being subsidiaries of Pearson Plc

PHOTOGRAPH ACKNOWLEDGEMENTS
Corbis: pp.1, 9, 11, 14, 16, 19, 29, 33, 34 and 35; Magnum: pp.6 and 25;
Topham: pp.20, 22, 27, 36 and 38.

For a complete list of the titles available in the Penguin Readers series please write to your
local Pearson Education office or to: Penguin Readers Marketing Department,
Pearson Education, Edinburgh Gate, Harlow, Essex CM20 2JE.

CONTENTS

INTRODUCTION

❝We must meet hate with love.**❞**

Martin Luther King, Jr. was one of America's greatest leaders. He was not a president, but his birthday is a national day in the US. Presidents are the only other Americans who are remembered in this way. King became famous around the world in the 1960s.

In the first half of the 1900s in the American South, African-Americans suffered terribly under white men's laws. King loved his country, but he hated these laws. He wanted an end to laws that were wrong. He wanted an end to segregation in the South. His dream was for black people and white people to live together peacefully. "All men are equal," he said. But in the US at that time, all men were not equal.

King had to change the way that people thought. His message of love had to change people's hearts and minds. It was a very difficult and dangerous plan. He led thousands of his black "brothers and sisters" in peaceful protests against the government. He led boycotts and protest marches. He taught African-Americans to use love against their enemies. Violence was always wrong.

People around the world read about King in the newspapers and saw him on TV. Many people were angry when they saw police violence against him and his followers. His peaceful fight for equality brought him pain and suffering. But he had a dream—for a better world for all people. African-Americans, and all Americans, have a better life today because of Martin Luther King, Jr. and the civil rights campaign.

"I HAVE A DREAM"

On August 28, 1963, Martin Luther King, Jr.* stood in front of more than 250,000 protest marchers in Washington, D.C. and gave one of the most famous speeches in US history. This protest march was the largest demonstration in the US at that time. About 60,000 marchers were white people; the other marchers were black. They came from all parts of the country into the nation's capital because they wanted change. They wanted equality for *all* Americans.

In the weeks before this march, the organizers invited important speakers. King worked on his speech all night, trying to find the right words. But the next day, in the middle of his speech, he changed it. He looked up at the crowd and spoke about his dream for America:

"I have a dream today . . . one day little black boys and little black girls will be able to join hands with little white boys and little white girls as sisters and brothers."

King's dream has not come true yet. But many Americans today have the same dream. His fight for peace, equality, and freedom for all people continues.

---

* Jr.: short for "Junior." This word is used after a man's name when he has the same name as his father.

KING'S EARLY LIFE

▌**THE BOY** Martin Luther King, Jr. was born on January 15, 1929, in Atlanta, Georgia in the American South. He was given his father's name—Michael. In 1934, after a trip to Germany, Daddy King changed his first name and his son's name to Martin. Martin Luther was the name of a great religious leader in Germany in the 1500s. Daddy King was a preacher and wanted to be like him. He wanted his son to be a great preacher one day, too.

Before King started school, he played with a little white boy. But at the age of five they had to go to different schools. Black children could not go to schools for whites. The white boy's parents told King to stop playing with their son. King went home crying. His parents explained to him about the difficult life for black people in the US. King decided then that he hated all white people.

In school, King loved sports, language, and reading books. The teachers moved him up a grade twice because he was very smart. He missed grades 9 and 11, and finished high school at the age of fifteen.

▌**FAMILY OF PREACHERS** King's grandfather—his mother's father—and his own father studied at Morehouse College for blacks in Atlanta and became Baptist* preachers at Atlanta's Ebenezer Baptist Church. This was the best job that a black man could have in the South. Daddy King was also a good businessman and an important leader of Atlanta's black population.

Religion was very important in King's early life. He went to church after school and all day on Sundays. At six, he began singing in the church while his mother played the piano.

*Baptist: the largest Protestant Christian group in the US

2

But when he was fifteen, he started to question the church's teachings. He did not want to become a preacher like his father. Daddy King was not happy about this.

At fifteen, King began studying at Morehouse College. The president of the college, Dr. Benjamin Mays, changed King's mind about many things—most importantly about his future. At seventeen, King decided to become a preacher. When he told his father, Daddy King tested his son. He told Martin to preach in his church the next Sunday. King was nervous, but he was a great success. Daddy King was very proud. King studied hard and on February 25, 1948, he became a preacher. Soon after that, he began working on Sundays at Ebenezer Church.

King graduated from Morehouse College in 1948 and continued his studies at a college for preachers near Philadelphia, Pennsylvania, in the North. After he graduated from there in 1951, he stayed in the North. He studied at one of the best colleges in Boston, Massachusetts. He graduated in 1955 as Dr. Martin Luther King.

Before graduation, he thought about the good life in the North. He could be a college professor. He liked the idea, but the poor black people in the South needed him. He could finish his college papers at night while he worked during the day. In January 1954, he returned to the segregated South. In his first job, at the Dexter Avenue Baptist Church in Montgomery, Alabama, King preached to the city's black doctors, teachers, and better-paid black people. There were 50,000 blacks and 90,000 whites in the city. Most of the blacks were very poor with low-paid jobs. King understood their pain and suffering. His church became their center for change.

FROM ENEMY TO FRIEND

King's opinions about white people changed as he grew up. When he was fifteen, he took a bus to a town in Georgia with a female teacher. There he won a prize for the best speech. On the way home they were happily talking when some white people got on the full bus. The driver told King and his teacher to give their seats to two white passengers. King refused. The driver spoke angrily and the teacher was afraid. She got up and told King to get up, too. They had to stand for two hours. "It was the angriest I have ever been in my life," King said later.

Then in 1945, Morehouse College sent some students north to work on a Connecticut farm for the summer. In Connecticut, King and his black friends could go to every restaurant. They used the front door entrance to theaters and chose their seats—like white people. But on the train back to Atlanta, a waiter took King to the back of the dining car. He pulled a cloth down in front of King's face because whites in the South hated to eat in the same room with a black man. King could not believe it. He was not angry now, just sad.

But his ideas changed even more after he learned about the teachings of Mahatma Gandhi. Gandhi, an Indian, told his people to love their enemies. This surprised King, but he agreed with Gandhi. One day a white college student pointed a gun at King and shouted angrily. But King did not become angry. He looked into the student's eyes and spoke calmly. Later, the student said sorry. This taught King an important lesson—how to change an enemy into a friend. After this, King was voted class president. He was growing from an angry boy to a forgiving young man—to a leader.

FROM SLAVERY TO FREEDOM

Daddy King wanted Martin to be proud of himself and his people. He sent Martin to good schools. He gave him a car when he went to college. King was very lucky and he knew it. Daddy King told Martin, "If you do not think like a slave, nobody can make you a slave."

■ HOW DID SLAVERY IN AMERICA START?

It began in 1620 after the first Europeans went to America by ship. These white people started big farms in the South and needed workers. Ship owners soon began to sail to Africa. They bought black people cheaply and took them back to America. There the Africans were sold as slaves. The slave-ship owners earned a lot of money from this. The first ship in 1620 carried twenty Africans, but by 1865 there were 4 million African slaves in the US. African men, women, and children had to work very hard for the white landowners. Some slaves escaped to the North and had a better life, but very few.

■ WHEN DID SLAVERY END?

It did not end until 1865. In 1807, President Thomas Jefferson tried to end slavery when he passed a new law. The use of slave-ships to America became illegal. But that did not stop the ship owners, and slavery continued for the next fifty-eight years.

■ WHY DID IT TAKE SO MANY YEARS?

Many people in the South did not want slavery to end. Slaves did their hard work for them. But many people in the North hated slavery. This difference of opinion became a big problem in the US. The states in the South wanted to leave the US and to start their own government. To stop them, the North fought the South in a great war from 1861–1865. More than 600,000 Americans died. After the North won, President Abraham Lincoln ended slavery.

■ HOW MUCH DID LIFE CHANGE IN THE SOUTH AFTER THE WAR?

African-Americans were now free—but many did not have jobs. They were poor and could not read or write. Rich landowners did not want black people to go to school. They were afraid of mixing with black people. "Black men will want to marry white women!" they said. So the white people in the South passed "Jim Crow" laws.

■ WHAT WERE JIM CROW LAWS?

These laws segregated black people from whites. Blacks had to live in the black part of town. They could not go to the white people's restaurants, hotels, churches, or schools. In 1896, the US government passed a law that accepted segregation in all states. Americans with dark skin had to sit in the back of city buses. They had to give their seats to white passengers when they wanted them. They could not drink

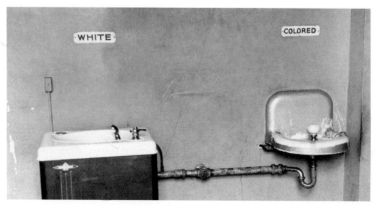

Black people could not drink the same water as whites.

the same drinking water. And they had to use the back entrance to theaters and sit upstairs. An intelligent black man, W.E.B. DuBois, started an organization in 1909, the NAACP.* This organization tried to change these laws.

■ WHAT EARLY SUCCESSES DID THE NAACP HAVE?

Successes were few, but on May 17, 1954, the US government finally passed a very important new law. Segregation in all US schools became illegal. The NAACP's long hard fight was a success! Many white people in the South were angry because this helped the civil rights campaign. For King and the NAACP, more changes were now possible.

■ HOW DID THE CIVIL RIGHTS CAMPAIGN START?

Work started with the NAACP, but the fight for civil rights for black people in white men's courts was almost impossible. For example, at the end of the Second World War in 1945, one million black US soldiers returned home. The US government gave money to white soldiers for houses. The black soldiers asked for the same help. They did not get it. They also wanted voting rights in the South. Segregationists made this almost impossible. Many blacks became angry. They did not fear white people and their laws as much as they did before. It was time to act—to protest. In December 1955, King became president of the MIA,* and the civil rights campaign of the 1950s and 1960s began. Now African-Americans had a man who could speak for them—Martin Luther King, Jr. At this time King became friends with Ralph Abernathy, another black preacher in Montgomery. These two preachers organized a thirteen-year campaign that changed the nation.

* NAACP: an organization that fought segregation laws in the courts
* MIA: an organization of black preachers and leaders in Montgomery, Alabama that protested against unfair laws in the city

THE KING FAMILY

King met Coretta Scott in 1952 while he was studying in Boston. She was from Alabama and, like King, loved the North. She was studying at a famous music school. This beautiful and intelligent singer was King's perfect wife. He told her this the first time they went out together. "I don't see how you can say that," she told him. "You don't even know me." But King knew what he wanted.

IMPORTANT DATES

June 18, 1953	King marries Coretta Scott
January 1954	They move to Montgomery, Alabama
November 17, 1955	Daughter Yolanda is born
October 23, 1957	Son Martin Luther King III is born
January 1961	Son Dexter is born
March 28, 1963	Daughter Bernice is born

In the first two years after their marriage, Coretta traveled around the country. She sang and gave the money to the civil rights campaign. But after she and Martin started a family, King wanted her to stay home. She became his secretary.

Coretta did not want to return to the South, but her husband's work was more important than a comfortable life. After they moved to Montgomery, she often worried about Martin. Many white people wanted to kill him. Often in her dreams at night, his life ended violently. Near the end of his life King said, "If anything happens to me, Coretta, you must . . . continue."

King was not able to spend a lot of time with Coretta and the children because the civil rights campaign took him around the country. But their hours and days together were very happy and very special.

Martin Luther King with his wife, Coretta, and children 'Marti' and Yolanda.

KING AND THE MONTGOMERY BUS BOYCOTT

In 1955, Martin and Coretta were living in the black part of Montgomery, Alabama. The people at Dexter Avenue Baptist Church liked their new young preacher and his ideas. King, and other black Montgomery preachers, wanted to protest against segregation on city buses.

Segregation in schools was illegal by that time, but segregation on buses in the South continued. Many blacks were angry, but what could they do? The black leaders of Montgomery knew that boycotts were helping blacks in Baton Rouge, Louisiana. They wanted to start a boycott in Montgomery, too.

But they knew that the courts did not help ordinary black men or women. They wanted the police to arrest a polite, quiet person with a good job. But who?

On Thursday December 1, 1955, a forty-year-old black woman, Mrs. Rosa Parks, finished work and went shopping. Then she got on a bus and sat down. She was tired and her feet hurt. By the next stop the bus was full. The bus driver told Mrs. Parks to give her seat to a white passenger. She refused. The bus driver called the police and they arrested Mrs. Parks.

Mrs. Parks was the secretary of E.D. Nixon, the NAACP worker for Montgomery and the state of Alabama. After her arrest, she phoned him. He paid her bail and she went home to her worried husband. Nixon was excited and phoned King. They finally had their special person. King, Nixon, and Abernathy organized a meeting of church leaders and other important black people. Mrs. Parks was an honest, smart woman and people in the city liked her. She bravely agreed to go to court and fight for her civil rights. A boycott of the Montgomery city buses began.

Rosa Parks rides the bus.

The next Thursday night, information about the boycott was secretly copied by a female college professor, and it was given to blacks around the city the next day. On Monday morning of December 5, 50,000 boycotters spoke with their feet: "We will not ride on segregated buses again!"

Also on Monday morning, Abernathy suggested a new organization, the MIA. The start of the boycott was a great success. But they needed a new organization with a strong leader to continue the boycott. All of the black leaders wanted King for president. King said, "Somebody has to do it. And if you think I can, I will …" Was he the right man for the job, he asked himself. Could he lead a civil rights campaign? The next few years proved that he could.

Black taxi companies offered cheap rides to the boycotters. Fifty black car-owners, and later some whites, helped. Almost no black person used the buses. The bus company and white politicians were angry because they were losing money. In Montgomery, almost three-quarters of the people on city buses were black. The politicians tried to stop the boycott. But King and the MIA worked endlessly to continue it.

Police in Montgomery wanted to destroy the boycott and King. On the night of January 26, 1956, they arrested King for driving two kilometers an hour faster than the correct speed for that street. King was surprised and afraid, but he did not protest. Abernathy led a crowd of black people to the jail. They wanted King. The police told King to go home.

On the evening of January 30, 1956, the KKK* bombed King's house. Luckily, Coretta and their baby, Yolanda, were not hurt. King hurried home and found hundreds of angry black people in front of his house. They wanted to attack the

* KKK: short for "Ku Klux Klan," a secret organization of white men who hated African-Americans

white policemen. Bravely, King told them, "I want you to go home. We must love our white brothers . . . We must meet hate with love." These people loved King, so they went home.

CAMPAIGN OF FEAR The KKK, started in 1865, was an organization of white men in the South. They wanted "White rule for America!" Dressed in white from head to foot, the KKK violently attacked black people at night. They bombed and burned black people's houses and churches. They killed black people and burned crosses in people's yards.

On February 21, the court in Montgomery decided to jail eighty-nine leaders of the boycott and all of the black car drivers. King was in Nashville, Tennessee, but he talked to Abernathy on the telephone. King went to Montgomery and joined the boycotters in jail on February 24, 1956. He had to pay $500 and court costs, but King was happy. Now more people read in the newspapers about the peaceful protests in Montgomery.

The next month, in April 1956, white city leaders told the MIA to stop the bus boycott. Boycotts became illegal. King knew what he had to do. He continued to boycott and was arrested again. He had to pay $500 bail, but his arrest became international news. World opinion was with King and the boycotters! King was famous.

After 381 days of the boycott, on November 3, 1956, the US government passed a new law—segregation on buses in all states was illegal! King, the MIA, and the black boycotters of Montgomery won the long, hard fight.

PEACEFUL FIGHTERS AGAINST VIOLENCE

Many of King's ideas about protest marches and boycotts came from Henry David Thoreau and Mahatma Gandhi. He read their books in college and liked their ideas.

▌ **THOREAU** (1817–1862) was a famous American writer from Concord, Massachusetts. In 1849, Thoreau bravely refused to pay money on his earnings to the US government. He disagreed with the US war with Mexico, and he did not want his money to pay for it. Thoreau was sent to jail for one night. After that, he wrote: There are some laws that are not right. Honest men must change them. Sometimes it is right for honest men to break the law. If a government does not stop the use of slaves, honest men must use peaceful protest against their government.

▌ **GANDHI** (1869–1948) had similar ideas. From him, King learned that men should love their enemies. They should fight violence with peace. Gandhi was born in India and studied law in England. In 1919 he started his first peaceful

protest against British rule in India. Then he led a boycott of British cloth and was sent to prison. As a freedom fighter, he spent 2,338 days in prison. He was famous around the world. As a result of his peaceful protests, India won its freedom in 1947. On January 30, 1948, Gandhi was murdered.

MONTGOMERY'S FAMOUS PREACHER

The year 1956 ended with terrible violence against blacks in Montgomery. The KKK was shooting at buses and burning crosses. On January 10, 1957, Abernathy's house and church were bombed. Other churches were bombed, too. When King and Abernathy visited them, they felt sick. They could not believe their eyes. "Was I wrong?" King asked himself. On King's twenty-eighth birthday, the worry weighed heavily on his heart. He cried as he spoke to the people in his church. "If someone must die, *I* will die," he said sadly. Later, he spoke about that day in church. "After that, I did not fear death," he said.

After the Montgomery boycott, King was asked to give speeches all over the country. He was offered good jobs. But King stayed at Dexter Avenue Baptist Church and led the MIA. He was ready to begin his next fight. He wanted voting rights for all African-American adults.

On March 3, 1957, King and his wife flew to Ghana, West Africa. Ghana was now free from British rule. The new leader invited King to visit. It was King's first visit to Africa and he learned a lot from it. He saw African people ruling their own country. He went to Nigeria and saw terrible suffering. He became very interested in Africa. He felt very close to his African brothers in their fight for freedom from foreign rule.

Back home, King wanted President Eisenhower to help the blacks in the South. But the President was not interested. King and Abernathy went to Washington and spoke to Richard Nixon, the closest man to the President. They wanted him to give a message to Eisenhower. Only the President could end segregation, they said. This visit changed nothing. Schools in the South were still segregated. Segregationists had criminal minds and easily broke laws. African-Americans in the South still had no voting rights. But King had an idea.

He called 115 black leaders to Montgomery on August 7 and 8, and they started a new organization, the SCLC.* Again King was voted for president. He worked very closely with three people from the North: Bayard Rustin, Stanley Levison, and Ella Baker. He needed their help because he was making speeches all over the country. While he traveled, they organized activities.

In February 1957, King's photo was on the cover of *Time* magazine. Called "The Man of the Year," King was becoming more popular. This was excellent for the campaign.

This famous photo of King was seen for the first time in the national newspapers on September 4, 1958. It surprised the readers of the earlier *Time* story. On September 3, King tried to go into a court room to speak to Abernathy. A guard angrily told King, "Boy, if you don't get away from here, *you* will need a lawyer!" Two policemen pulled King's arm behind his back and took him to jail. A newspaper photographer took a photo. The police

* SCLC: an organization in the South to help African-Americans get voting rights

soon discovered that this black man was King. They politely sent him home. But it was too late and newspapers printed the photo of police violence against King. Many Americans were very surprised and angry. King was told to pay $10 or go to jail. He chose fourteen days in jail. "I make this decision because of my love for America . . . " he said in court. But the Chief of Police paid the $10. He now understood—King's arrests were good for his campaign.

About three weeks later, on September 20, King was signing copies of his first book in Blumstein's store in Harlem, New York. A black woman walked in and nearly killed King with a knife. After the attack, King was weak for some months. But he forgave the woman and did not take her to court. He received cards and messages from people around the world.

On November 29, 1959, King decided to leave Dexter Avenue Baptist Church. He needed more time for civil rights work. He decided to work with his father at Ebenezer Church in Atlanta again. Before he left, on February 1, 1960, Montgomery's black leaders had a special goodbye party for King. On that same day in North Carolina, a group of black students began their own, new peaceful protest. The results surprised everyone.

■ STUDENT PROTESTS On February 1, 1960, four black college students from Greensboro, North Carolina, sat down at the lunch bar in the Woolworth's store. They ordered their food politely. They were told to leave. Lunch bars were for "WHITES ONLY." They refused to go. Their brave protest was the start of many student demonstrations at lunch bars across the South. On February 13, in Nashville,

Tennessee, 500 students walked in and sat down at lunch bars. At Orangeburg, South Carolina, police arrested 388 college students. In March, students demonstrated in forty cities. The country was getting very nervous. In the year 1960, a total of 70,000 African-American students demonstrated.

Many people thought that King started these demonstrations. But it was not true. His work led the way, and others followed the path of peaceful protest.

■ KING GOES TO PRISON The student organization SNCC* wanted King to march with them and sit down at the lunch bar in Rich's. This was Atlanta's largest store. But King was very busy with meetings and speeches. The students continued asking him. Finally, he agreed.

On October 19, 1960, the police arrested King with thirty-five students at Rich's lunch bar. They refused bail and were sent to prison. Surprisingly, for their first meal behind bars, they were given steak. The reason was clear—the world was watching. World opinion was again with King and the demonstrators. This brought big problems to the owner of Rich's and to the city of Atlanta.

One of the city's judges, Judge Mitchell, wanted to keep King in prison. He sent the students home on October 25, but not King. The next morning the prison officers took King to DeKalb Jail. Mitchell hated blacks and wanted to silence their leader. He gave King four months in prison. In the early hours of the next morning, the police drove King 500 kilometers through dark country roads. "Are they going to kill me?" he thought. They took him to Reidsville State Prison for the worst criminals. There King phoned his worried wife. He was worried, too.

* SNCC: an organization of young, black college students similar to the SCLC

■ FREE MARTIN LUTHER KING!
The front page of the newspapers reported on King's move to Reidsville. Coretta phoned King's lawyer. After he made a few phone calls, John F. Kennedy—"JFK"—phoned Coretta. He offered to help. Kennedy was a famous politician, campaigning for the job of President of the US. Coretta was grateful to JFK and accepted his offer. JFK talked to Judge Mitchell on October 27, and King was freed on $2,000 bail.

Daddy King was also grateful to JFK. He brought his son back to Ebenezer Church and spoke to the crowd.

JFK—the 35th US President.

"Don't vote for Richard Nixon," he said. "Vote for JFK!" King was grateful to JFK, too, but he did not try to get votes for him. "I am not a politician," King said.

In November 1960, Kennedy received 34,221,463 votes and Nixon 34,108,582. JFK became the 35th US President in January 1961. Two phone calls about a black preacher in an Alabama prison helped him to win.

■ **FREEDOM RIDES** These became another way for black students to protest against segregation in bus stations across the South. They were joined by a small number of white people. On May 4, 1961, the "Freedom Riders" rode Greyhound buses to bus stations and sat down in "WHITES ONLY" seats. Over the next few months, Freedom Rides resulted in some of the nation's worse violence during the civil rights years.

On May 15, a Freedom Ride bus was attacked by about 200 KKK men. They threw a firebomb into the bus near Anniston, Alabama. When the passengers ran out of the burning bus, the KKK hit them with heavy sticks. The Freedom Riders were kicked, and some were covered in blood. A photographer took a photo of the burning bus, and it was printed in national and international newspapers. Americans across the country were very angry.

Another bus was arriving in Birmingham immediately after this one. The police wanted to help the KKK. They gave them fifteen minutes to attack the Freedom Riders. Blacks and whites were very badly hurt and were taken to the hospital. The KKK followed and angrily attacked them again inside the hospital.

The famous burning bus, Anniston, May 15, 1961.

On May 19, a very large crowd of segregationists attacked the Freedom Riders in Montgomery. Robert Kennedy, JFK's brother, sent 400 US soldiers to stop the riot. No one was killed but many people were hurt. King flew into Montgomery. That evening, he was giving a speech to 1,500 people inside Abernathy's church. A large crowd of angry segregationists stood outside, shouting. There were some soldiers protecting the church from the crowd. When rocks were thrown through the church windows, the soldiers used gas against the crowd. King was very worried and he phoned Robert Kennedy. Kennedy promised to send more soldiers. But before he could, the state leader sent Alabama's National Guard and police. At 4.30 A.M., the National Guard began to move people out of the church.

The Freedom Riders finally reached their goal. On September 22, segregation in bus stations in the South ended.

WE WON'T LET BLACKS IN!

When segregation in schools became illegal in 1954, African-Americans had new hope for the future. But the segregationists in the South did not want the US government to change their way of life. On September 4, 1957, nine black students tried to go to a white high school in Little Rock, Arkansas. Orval Faubus, the state leader, sent the National Guard to stop them. President Eisenhower had to stop Faubus breaking the laws of the US government. He sent 1,000 soldiers. Under their protection, the black students went inside.

But the President's actions did not stop other segregationists. In September 1962, James Meredith, an African-American, wanted to study at a famous Mississippi college for whites. When he tried to go to classes, a riot started. Two people were killed and 375 were hurt. President Kennedy sent soldiers. The next morning the soldiers protected Meredith when he went to classes. But whites refused to sit near him.

In 1962, George Wallace became state leader of Alabama. He promised to continue segregation in the state colleges. "I will personally stand in the schoolhouse door!" And he did exactly that. On June 11, 1963, two African-Americans tried to go to an Alabama college. Again Kennedy had to send the National Guard to protect them.

James Meredith

THE COUNTRY'S MOST SEGREGATED CITY

Birmingham, Alabama ruled its black population by fear in the 1950s and 1960s. King wanted to take his campaign there for one reason—to stop Bull Connor. The city's police chief, Eugene "Bull" Connor, hated black people and their civil rights campaign. King and Fred Shuttlesworth were his biggest enemies. Shuttlesworth was a black preacher in Birmingham and he worked hard for civil rights. After the KKK bombed his home and church on Christmas night, 1956, he asked King to come to Birmingham. He needed the famous leader's help.

King and Abernathy worked closely together. They led meetings and demonstrations. Hundreds of protesters were arrested. The SCLC bailed them out of jail. Then on April 11, 1963, the Alabama state court sent a letter to King and Abernathy. It was now illegal for blacks to demonstrate in Alabama. King spoke to reporters in front of television cameras. "The court will not stop me," he told them. The next day, the police arrested King, Abernathy, and fifty demonstrators and put them in Birmingham Jail. This was King's thirteenth time in jail, but this jail was worse than Reidsville Prison. King was very worried.

On April 16, King's lawyers secretly brought King a newspaper, the *Birmingham News*. In it, eight white preachers disagreed with King and his campaign. He decided to write a long letter to them. He wanted to explain his goals carefully. His lawyers secretly brought him a pen. King wrote on the newspaper because he did not have writing paper. When the letter became very long, he continued it on paper from the bathroom.

■ **LETTER FROM BIRMINGHAM JAIL** King wrote: Why do you hate the demonstrations, but you do not hate the reasons for them? For years the black man has heard the word "Wait!" but it has nearly always meant "*Never*." America's black people have waited for more than 340 years. White people kill black mothers and fathers. Policemen kill our black brothers and sisters. What will happen next? We never know. When you understand our problems, you will also understand this. We find it difficult to wait.

King's lawyers secretly took the letter out of the jail. It was printed as a small book and sent to churches. A copy was sent to Robert Kennedy and to other politicians in Washington. Not one of the eight preachers ever answered King's letter but it has become famous in protest literature.

Eight days after their arrest, King and Abernathy paid $300 bail. They left jail, but they were worried. They needed new ideas. The next few days made history in the civil rights campaign.

■ **THE CHILDREN'S MARCH** There were plans for a protest march and Birmingham's black children wanted to march, too. King agreed, and for the next few weeks there was war on the streets of Birmingham.

On May 2, 1963, adult protesters led more than 1,000 children from the Sixteenth Street Baptist Church toward downtown. Bull Connor told the police to arrest the children—and they did. More than 600 African-American children were arrested; some were only six years old.

The next day, 2,500 children marched again. Bull Connor gave the order and the city's firemen attacked the children with water. It crashed into them and knocked them down. Police dogs ran after some marchers and bit them. Many people were hurt and 250 were arrested. Americans, and people around the world, watched on TV and could not believe their eyes. President Kennedy watched the violence on TV, too. He said, "The black people of Birmingham are tired of being patient. I can understand why."

Birmingham's firemen attack black protesters with water.

King told the children's parents, "Don't worry about your children in jail. They are suffering so they can make this nation a better nation. If they want some books, we will get them. I read a lot every time I go to jail."

The brave African-Americans of Birmingham continued to march. Police continued to use water and dogs. There were more arrests. Then on May 5, Bull Connor again ordered the firemen to turn on the water. But this time they did nothing. He was wrong and they knew it. The blacks continued to march past. For the first time, King saw strong, proud protesters in Birmingham.

Police continued to arrest marchers. On May 6, more than 3,000 African-Americans filled the jails. This was success! This was King's dream. "What can the police do now?" he thought. "They will have to do something." On May 10, King and the SCLC made an agreement with important business and church leaders in Birmingham. Things were getting better, they thought.

Then on May 11, King's brother, A.D., phoned King. A.D.'s house and a hotel in Birmingham were bombed the night before. The KKK thought that King was in the hotel. But they were wrong. He was home in Atlanta for Mother's Day. A riot started and JFK sent soldiers.

Finally, there was good news. On May 23, Bull Connor lost his job. The voters did not want him. The words WHITE and COLORED disappeared from lunch bars, bathrooms, and drinking-water machines. Some black people were employed in the stores downtown.

■ HOW DID BIRMINGHAM CHANGE THE NATION? The world was watching and reporting on Dr. Martin Luther King, Jr. and the peaceful protests. President Kennedy began preparing a new civil rights bill. On June 11, he gave an important speech to the American people. Every man has the right to enjoy equal service and the right to vote, he said. It was time for America to change. But not all Americans agreed with their President. After JFK's speech that night, a segregationist shot and killed the famous NAACP worker Medgar Evers in Jackson, Mississippi.

King wanted Kennedy and his government to change more laws. But Kennedy was worried. He did not want another war between the South and the North.

Speaking at a meeting in Birmingham on June 20, King

said, "I think we should march on Washington with a quarter of a million people." He told Kennedy his plan. There will be no violence, he promised. But on the day of the march, Kennedy put 4,000 soldiers outside Washington. Hospitals were told to prepare. Bayard Rustin and the SCLC organized the march.

▎ THE MARCH ON WASHINGTON   One hundred "Freedom Buses" drove into the city every hour that day. Twenty-one "Freedom Trains" brought marchers from all parts of the US. An eighty-two-year-old man came by bike from Ohio. A younger man rode his bike from South Dakota. An airplane from Hollywood brought movie stars like Marlon Brando. Bob Dylan and Joan Baez arrived and sang to the crowd. More than 200,000 marchers arrived in the nation's capital; almost one quarter of them were white. For the first time, white and black Americans stood together as one nation.

Just before King gave his speech, America's three biggest TV stations stopped the afternoon programs. All of America was watching when King walked on stage. Millions of people around the world heard his loud clear voice: "I have a dream . . . " His dream for the future was for all children, all Americans. The color of a person's skin did not matter. Only a person's heart and mind were important.

The crowd loved King's speech. They shouted happily when Rustin spoke about the purpose of the march. They wanted no more segregation in schools, higher pay, and more jobs for African-Americans. Morehouse College President, Benjamin Mays said the final words and the march ended.

Later, King was very happy. After his speech, he and some of the other speakers went to JFK's office. The President shook King's hand and said, "*I* have a dream!"

DEATH OF A PRESIDENT JFK was riding through the streets of Dallas, Texas, on November 22, 1963, when he was shot dead. Lyndon Baines Johnson—LBJ—became the next President.

Eighteen days after King gave his "I Have a Dream" speech, three KKK men bombed the Sixteenth Street Baptist Church in Birmingham. Four young school girls were killed. Police arrested one man, then freed him. King went immediately to Birmingham and talked to the people. He could not explain this terrible act. The court was in no hurry to send the criminals to prison. One of the bombers, Robert Chambliss, was not sent to prison for this crime until 1977. A second bomber, Herman Cash, never went to court and died in 1994. The third bomber, Bobby Frank Cherry, was finally sent to prison in June 2002.

THE YOUNGEST NOBEL PEACE PRIZE WINNER

On December 10, 1964, at the age of 35, Martin Luther King, Jr. accepted the Nobel Peace Prize* in Stockholm, Sweden. He was the youngest winner in history. But he did not accept it for himself. He accepted it for all of the peaceful protesters against segregation and inequality around the world.

The next day, he spoke at a college in Norway. Black people and poor people cannot stay poor for ever, he said. Ten million American families are poor. They know they live in the richest nation on earth. It is time to fight for poor people. Rich nations must help poor nations.

And he spoke about war. War is not the way to solve problems, he said. It is necessary to end war and violence between nations. We can solve problems through peaceful activities.

After King received the Nobel Prize, he was Atlanta's most famous person. Dr. Mays organized a big, expensive dinner for him with 1,500 people. The KKK planned to bomb the hotel, but the police stopped them. The dinner was a success. White city leaders sat down and ate with black city leaders. This was another part of King's dream.

Martin Luther King accepts the Nobel Peace Prize.

* Nobel Peace Prize: a prize for the hard work of the world's best leaders

KING WANTS VOTING RIGHTS NOW!

In the South, most African-American adults could not vote. Segregationists did not want voting rights for blacks because they did not want black politicians. The segregationists gave reading and writing tests to the blacks who wanted to vote. But the tests were impossible. Most blacks failed the tests, so they could not vote.

In 1965, Selma, Alabama had an adult population of almost 30,000. Half were black but only 333 of them could vote. The worst segregationist states of Alabama, Louisiana, and Mississippi did not have voting rights for blacks. King decided to organize protest marches in Selma.

They began on January 18, 1965, when he led 400 blacks to the courthouse. King politely asked to put the marchers' names on the voting list. They were told to leave. They marched to a big hotel. Black people walked through its entrance for the first time. There, they signed their names to the voting list. This was a very small step toward success.

As the marchers went toward the courthouse on January 25, 1965, the city's law officers violently attacked a female marcher. Photographers were waiting for this and took photos for the nation's newspapers.

On February 1, police arrested King, Abernathy, and 250 marchers. Inside jail, King continued to give orders to the marchers through his assistant, Andrew Young. Marches continued the next day, February 2. That afternoon, 500 schoolchildren were arrested. This did not stop the marchers. Police arrested 3,000 people and put them in jail.

King's arrest was in all of the newspapers across the country. Television news reporters arrived in Selma. King was excited because everyone was interested in his campaign. President Johnson spoke about it on television and promised voting rights for all Americans.

King decided to write a letter to the *New York Times*. In his "Letter from a Selma Jail" on February 5, he wrote, "There are more blacks in jail with me than there are on the voting lists in Selma." The government was unhappy about this and sent a group of politicians to Selma. That same day, King paid his bail money and left jail.

He met President Johnson on February 9. LBJ promised to introduce a new civil rights law. But on February 10, a group of student marchers were violently attacked in Selma. As a result, King led 2,800 angry blacks on the biggest march of the campaign. They were met with more violence from whites. Newspapers and television reported it. Americans were sick of these pictures of violence.

On February 18, student marchers saw worse violence when a policeman's gun killed a young black man in front of his mother and father.

On March 5, protesters decided to march without King. He was in Atlanta. The police violence was worse than in Birmingham. News reports on TV and on radio called that day "Bloody Sunday." Protest marches and demonstrations were happening around the country because Americans, blacks and whites, were angry. King asked the protesters to come to Selma and help him fight segregation. Many answered his call.

Changes to civil rights laws could not happen quickly, and state leaders from the South voted against them. But finally, on March 15, President Johnson asked his government to pass the new Voting Rights law.

■ **THE SELMA TO MONTGOMERY MARCH** On March, 21, 3,200 people started marching from Selma. They were led by King. For five days, they marched. They wanted George Wallace, the Alabama state leader, to listen to them. They wanted voting rights and an end to police violence. Wallace refused to protect the marchers. So President Johnson had to send 3,900 soldiers and 100 FBI* men. Many people watched the marchers, but there was no violence along the way. At night the marchers slept in tents. Their feet hurt, but their hearts were full of happiness.

As they arrived outside Montgomery, it began to rain heavily. But when they marched into the city, the sun shone brightly. That night they slept in a city park.

The next day, March 25, they marched past Dexter Avenue Baptist Church. This brought back many memories for King and his wife. "It was a great [time] to go back to Montgomery . . . after ten years," Coretta Scott King said later. This time, the marchers were from different religions and a lot of them were white people. "It was really a beautiful thing . . . marching together," Coretta said.

King marched up the steps of the state building with other proud African-Americans. Rosa Parks of the Montgomery bus boycott was one. George Wallace refused to come out of the building. He did not want to listen to King and his followers. But King proudly spoke to the crowd. Black Americans will vote freely in their country soon, he said.

As a result of the protest marches, President Johnson signed the new Voting Rights law on August 6, 1965. Rosa Parks and Martin Luther King, Jr. stood next to him in the President's Room in the nation's capital.

* FBI: a government organization that uses spies to get information about enemies of the US

Selma to Montgomery marchers led by Martin Luther King, Jr. and Coretta.

DEFENDERS OF VIOLENCE

King's peaceful marches gave African-Americans a way to protest. But they paid a terrible price: violence and many deaths. Peaceful protests grew more and more unpopular with young blacks by the middle of the 1960s. They wanted more changes faster. King was talking about voting rights, but they wanted better houses and better jobs. Many young African-Americans in the North and in the South stopped listening to King. They began listening to other men with a very different message.

Malcolm X

■ MALCOLM X was a leader of the African-American organization called the Nation of Islam. Malcolm Little changed his last name to "X"—a sign of his lost African name. He told blacks to fight for their own state. They were African and they did not have to live with whites. He saw the need for a war for land. He spoke on TV and radio against King's peaceful protests. He told blacks to defend themselves with guns against the enemy. He believed that the March on Washington was organized by white politicians. King was hurt and worried about Malcolm X's ideas.

When Malcolm X left the Nation of Islam in 1964, the organization hated him. On February 21, 1965, three Nation of Islam men shot and killed him in Manhattan.

Stokely Carmichael

■ STOKELY CARMICHAEL was the new leader of the SNCC in 1966. He was called "the new Malcolm X" in the nation's newspapers. Carmichael started working for the SNCC in 1961 as a Freedom Rider. He spoke with clear, strong words. "Black is beautiful," he told America. His message to blacks was clear: "If you want freedom, you will have to take it from the whites!"

Carmichael liked King, but he did not agree with him. King's call for blacks and whites to work together was impossible. King was very worried. Carmichael and his followers were prepared for violence, but King did not want more riots.

More and more blacks were against King's peaceful protests. He was hurt, but he tried to understand their problems. For years he gave them hope and dreams, but nothing was happening. Their lives were not better. In some ways their lives were worse. But their rioting in the streets was not the answer, King thought.

RIOTS, WAR, AND TROUBLE

In 1965, America was getting deeper into a war in Asia. The US was helping South Vietnam fight a war against North Vietnam. In March 1965, President Johnson sent more soldiers and by June 1966, there were 125,000 US soldiers there. US bombs were killing a lot of Vietnamese people. "The war in Vietnam must stop," King said. Johnson was very angry at him for giving his opinion.

In their own country, African-Americans were angry and ready for a war against whites. Their lives were getting worse, not better. They were poor and there was no hope. From August 11–16, 1965, America's worst riot destroyed much of Watts, a very poor part of Los Angeles. It was started by a group of young black men. Thirty-four blacks were killed, 900 were hurt, and 3,500 were arrested. King arrived and saw the burned buildings and businesses. He went to the city leaders and explained the reasons for the rioters' actions. Almost one-third of the blacks in Watts had no jobs, he said. People had terrible houses. The city leaders did not agree with King.

Firemen fight a fire in Watts, Los Angeles, August 13, 1965.

Next, King went to Chicago and saw the homes for poor blacks in the city's worst areas. King wanted better houses for blacks. The city leader did not listen to King and there were terrible riots. Young black men used firebombs and guns against the police. On August 5, King led marchers through the white areas of the city. Whites threw rocks at the marchers and one hit King. A knife was thrown at King, but missed him. When King planned his next march, the city leader finally changed his mind. They made an agreement for better houses for blacks. But when King left Chicago, he felt very sad. Most white people there did not want to help blacks.

In the fall of 1967, there were more than 350,000 soldiers fighting in Vietnam. The US was spending $20 million a year on the war. A lot of Americans were protesting against their government's actions in the war. King continued his attacks. He told the SCLC to vote against President Johnson. The angry President wanted to destroy King. He told the FBI to get information about King's private life. They taped King's telephone calls and put tape recorders in his hotel rooms. Freedom of speech did not exist for him now. King's life was in great danger and he knew it.

In March 1967, the KKK bombed more churches in the South. Carmichael called for blacks to fight back and to kill the whites. Many African-Americans followed his orders. In the summer of 1967, there were riots in more than one hundred cities. King did not agree with violence, but he understood the rioters' feelings. He wrote to Johnson and told him to end unemployment. Johnson did not listen.

There were 35 million poor people in America. King wanted the government to give jobs to the poor. He began organizing a Poor People's Campaign—another march into Washington. Sadly, his life was ended before he could lead the campaign.

KING IS MURDERED

On the stormy evening of April 3, 1968, in Memphis, Tennessee, King gave his last speech. He was speaking to workers who wanted higher pay from the city. The city refused so the men stopped working.

King told them, "The nation is sick." He spoke about the urgent need for peace. There are difficult days in front of us, he said. "But it doesn't really matter with me now, because I've been to the mountaintop . . . and I've seen the Promised Land!* . . . I want you to know that we, as a people, will get to the Promised Land. And I'm happy tonight. I'm not worried about anything. I'm not fearing *any* man."

The last photograph of King, outside room 306 at the Memphis Hotel

* Promised Land: Good Christians believe that they will go to this place after death.

King spent much of the next day with Abernathy. That evening, they were getting ready to go out to dinner with friends. Waiting for Abernathy, King went outside of room 306 of the hotel. He joked with friends in the parking lot below. At six o'clock, a gunshot was heard. King was hit in the face. Abernathy ran to his friend and tried to stop the blood. King was taken to the hospital, but died at 7.05 P.M. on April 4, 1968.

Americans could not believe the news. Stokely Carmichael told blacks, "This is an act of war! Get your gun!" There were riots in 110 cities and 39 people were killed. On Monday April 8, Abernathy, Coretta and her three older children led a silent march of black workers through Memphis. On April 17, the workers won their fight for higher pay. King's work there was done.

On April 9, Abernathy spoke to 800 people inside Ebenezer Church. They were there to say goodbye to King. Coretta sat in front, dressed in black, with the four children. About 80,000 people stood outside. One hundred and twenty million Americans watched on TV.

The FBI found the killer's gun and they got a description of a white man. James Earl Ray was arrested on June 8 in London's Heathrow Airport. He was a criminal and hated blacks. Ray was sent to prison for thirty years for King's murder. But did he act alone? Many people think that he was working for others. But this is still an unsolved mystery today.

AFRICAN-AMERICANS TODAY

There are now African-Americans, like Colin Powell and Condoleeza Rice, in high government jobs. Black actors and actresses, like Denzel Washington and Halle Berry, have won the country's highest prizes for their acting. When Michael Anderson was a small boy, he dreamed of space travel. Years later, before *Columbia* crashed in 2003, he was doing scientific tests in space. His death on Columbia was very sad, but African-Americans are now beginning to live their dreams.

But do African-Americans have equality with white Americans? A black person earns fifty-seven cents for every dollar that a white person earns. Police stop African-American drivers on the roads seven times more often than other drivers. Police violence against blacks in American cities is seen on TV too often.

A lot has changed for African-Americans since the 1960s, but King's dream has not yet come true. Equality, peace, and love are in the hearts and minds of many people today. But hate and violence still stand in the way of their dream for a better America and a better world.

Since his death, Americans have become more and more grateful for King's fight for civil rights. We can visit the Martin Luther King Jr. Center in Atlanta and the National Civil Rights Center in Memphis. Today in the US African-Americans, and their white brothers and sisters, remember Dr. Martin Luther King, Jr. every third Monday in January. His birthday is the only national day for an American who was not a president. Coretta King's dream of a Martin Luther King Day came true on November 2, 1983, after fifteen years of trying.

MARTIN LUTHER KING DAY

Martin Luther King Day is a very special day. Banks, schools, and offices are closed on every national day. But Americans spend a lot of time preparing for Martin Luther King Day.

People in every state around the country remember King with a day of service in their towns and cities. King realized that service to other people was a great equalizer. So Americans help the poor, the sick, the homeless, and old people on this day. They do not go to work, but they do work for the local people in their towns.

There are also special ways to remember King in churches. Preachers from different religions join together and speak about King and his work. People in the churches sing the songs that were popular with protest marchers.

Almost everybody understands the need to teach children about equality. In schools across the US teachers prepare school children for Martin Luther King Day. Children learn about King and the civil rights campaign. They have special classes on African-American history. They prepare plays about important people, like Rosa Parks.

In New York City some schoolchildren prepare a march every year to important places of the civil rights years. The children prepare speeches to read at each of these places. Some years they stop at Blumstein's store: King was almost killed there while he was signing his books.

Coretta Scott King and her children keep King's memory alive. In January 1993, Dexter Scott King wrote, "My father died at age thirty-nine. But he lived a life fuller than most people." This life is gone but not forgotten.

ACTIVITIES

Pages 1 – 13

Before you read

1   What do you know about the history of African-Americans? What do you know about Martin Luther King, Jr.?

2   Find these words in your dictionary. They are all used in this book. Which are words for:

   a people?

   b people's actions against their government?

   c criminal actions?

   bomb   boycott   campaign   demonstrate   leader   march preacher   protest   slave   violence

3   Find these words in your dictionary and use them in sentences.

   a *arrest, bail, jail*

   b *peace, equality, freedom*

   c *segregate, civil rights, voting rights*

4   Read the Introduction. Are these sentences true or not? Correct the sentences that are not true.

   a King was only famous in the US.

   b There were unfair laws against black Americans in the South.

   c King did not like these laws and led protests against them.

   d King taught African-Americans to love violence.

   e The civil rights campaign changed the lives of many Americans.

After you read

5   Discuss the reasons for slavery and segregation in the US. Was there slavery in your country or a country near yours?

6   Answer these questions.

   a What did King's early life teach him about segregation and white people?

b How did the arrests of Rosa Parks and Martin Luther King help the civil rights campaign?

Pages 14 – 28

Before you read

7 How did white people from the North and white people from the South feel about King in the late 1950s and early 1960s? Why?

8 Find the word *riot* in your dictionary. Describe a riot that happened in your country or in a country near yours. How and why did it start? Who was there? Was anybody hurt? How did it end?

After you read

9 What did King learn from reading Thoreau and Gandhi? How did these writers help King in his fight for equality?

10 What do you know about these people?

    a The KKK and the Freedom Riders

    b President Eisenhower and Orval Faubus

    c George Wallace and Bull Connor

    d John F. Kennedy and Robert Kennedy

    e Ralph Abernathy and Bayard Rustin

11 King was taken to Reidsville Prison for the worst criminals. From there, he phoned his wife. Work with another student. Act the conversation between them.

Pages 29 – 41

Before you read

12 Look at the photos in this part of the book. Discuss them with another student. What is happening, do you think?

13 Read the titles on the Contents page for these pages. What do you think they are about?

After you read

14 What happened on:

   a December 10, 1964?

   b March 5, 1965?

   c August 6, 1965?

   d February 21, 1965?

   e August 11–16, 1965?

15 Who said this? Explain what they were talking about.

   a "It was really a beautiful thing . . . marching together."

   b "If you want freedom, you will have to take it from the whites."

   c "The war in Vietnam must stop."

   d "I'm not fearing *any* man."

Writing

16 Write your own "I Have a Dream" speech. What do you hope will happen in the future in your country or in the world?

17 Do you agree with King's idea of peaceful protests and law-breaking? Are these the right way to make changes? Write your opinion for a newspaper.

18 Do you think there is equality between blacks and whites in the US today? Find more information about this and write a letter to the US President.

19 Write ten questions for Coretta Scott King about her life before and after her husband's death.

Answers for the activities in this book are available from your local
Pearson Education Office.
Alternatively, write to: Penguin Readers Marketing Department,
Pearson Education, Edinburgh Gate, Harlow, Essex CM20 2JE.
Also visit www.penguinreaders.com for your free Factsheet for this book.